"In the long run we shape our lives and we shape ourselves. The process never ends until we die. And the choices we make are ultimately our own responsibility."

—Eleanor Roosevelt

Life's Finishing School: What Now?

A Ninety-Year-Old's View of Life and Living a Good Life

*See Reverse Side of the Book for
A Ninety-Year-Old's View
of Death and Dying
a Good Death*

by
Helen Green Ansley

Illustrations by Marion Weber

**Conscious Living / Conscious Dying:
A Project of the Institute of Noetic Sciences**

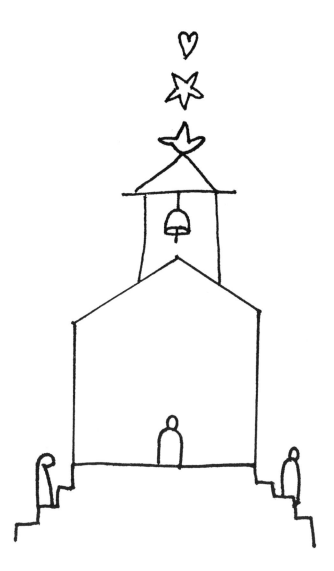

I see life as a Finishing School, the Ultimate Finishing School, with a full curriculum that teaches us Conscious Living, so that we may graduate—with honors—with a Conscious Death.

—*Helen Ansley*

For permission to reprint portions of this work contact
Institute of Noetic Sciences
475 Gate Five Road, Suite 300
Box 909
Sausalito, CA 94966-0909
(415) 331-5650

Produced for the Institute of Noetic Sciences
by Carol Guion
with the help of Sharon Skolnick and Lisa Mertz

Cover design: Carol Guion
Charts design: Helen Ansley
Cover and charts production art: Sharon Skolnick

Special thanks to Noel Andrews, Violet Cleveland,
Laura Franklin and Stephen Jamison for their contributions

Printed by United Graphics of Indiana, Inc., Terre Haute

ISBN 0-943951-01-1

Price $7.50
$6.60 to members of the Institute of Noetic Sciences

Any additional gifts will go directly to the Institute's
Conscious Living/Conscious Dying Project,
and are tax-deductible.

Contents

Life's Finishing School: What Now?
A Ninety-Year-Old's View
of Life and Living
a Good Life

See reverse side of the book for
Life's Finishing School: What Next?
A Ninety-Year-Old's View
of Death and Dying
a Good Death

8 Introduction: Winston O. Franklin
9 Foreword: Ken Dychtwald
10 A Note from the Illustrator: Marion Weber
12 Prologue: There is a Thread:
       Suzannah Arnold
14 Helen Green Ansley:
       The Pattern of a Century
19 Life's Finishing School:
       A Curriculum for Living Well
29   • The A's and The FFIG's:
          Psychobabble Translated
59   • Growing Wise to Ourselves
93   • A New Image of Aging

Introduction
by Winston O. Franklin

Helen Ansley is an "outrageous" elder, and her willingness at age ninety to challenge our society's prevailing myths surrounding aging, death, and dying is refreshing. These issues seem at once both the same and very different: one's simply "finishing life" and wishing to "graduate" as contrasted with one's confronting a terminal disease at an earlier stage of life.

Both because of our aging population and the scourge of the AIDS epidemic, death and the dying process is a timely subject on the consciousness agenda. The Institute of Noetic Sciences has established the Conscious Living/ Conscious Dying Project as a means for exploration and further learning in this area.

Most Institute publications have a visionary research base. This book is an exception, as it represents the very personal views of a single member. It is an exception we make readily in order to communicate more widely the timely message of this exceptional "Elder" who has won our hearts.

"Wink" Franklin is Executive Vice-President of the Institute of Noetic Sciences, on its Board and on the Steering Committee of its Conscious Living / Conscious Dying Project.

Foreword
by Ken Dychtwald, PhD

I met Helen Ansley back in 1974, when she was a participant in our first SAGE group, and now, many years later, she is a consultant to my company Age Wave, Inc. Helen is a perfect illustration that growing old isn't what it used to be. We're now living longer, with more health, vigor and social involvement than at any other time in history.

With 30 vital years added to human life expectancy, as has occurred during the past century, we now have a choice between growing old as we always have, with an additional two to three decades of old age tagged to the end, or practicing *a new way of living.*

Extended life need not mean extended old age. Rather, it offers an elongation of the periods of life we most enjoy—extra years of youthful adventure, a slowed down middle age, a length-ened late adulthood filled with new experiences and satisfactions, and a vigorous old age. What many of us call aging is frequently a lifestyle issue instead. With optimal care, we now know that it is possible to grow old *well* with energy and vigor. And Helen Ansley is a prime example of someone growing old well.

A Note From The Illustrator
by Marion Weber

It is my sincere hope that these illustrations will help stimulate *your* imagination and *your* visions around dying well and living well.

We are all artists blessed with awesome imaginations. The only things holding us back are fear and judgment.

So let these two feelings go and breathe in playfulness, trust, spontaneity and a spirit of adventure. And see what emerges!

Here is a list of what's needed in order to explore with your imagination:

1. one hour
2. a space that feels safe and comfortable
3. willingness
4. openness
5. relaxed body
6. music
7. tools (paper, pencils, etc.)

Begin by closing your eyes. Feel your body completely held by the Earth. Visualize spirit energy like a gentle cape resting on your head, shoulders and arms. Visualize a warm protective circle around you. Feel your pulse in your hands.

Now pick up a pencil and with your eyes still closed let your hand move spontaneously across the paper, trusting your own rhythm. Open your eyes. See if the lines suggest anything to you.

Now with the same totally relaxed free manner open your imagination concerning some subject, some aspect of life or death. Sit with that subject, open to receiving an image about it. When the image comes, lovingly draw it. There is no right way to draw it. There is no wrong way to draw it. Only your way.

Be surprised!
Have fun!
Enjoy your beautiful imagination.
It is a gift!
Share it with a friend!

Artist Marion Weber is on the Board of Directors of the Institute of Noetic Sciences, and on the Steering Committee of its Conscious Living/Conscious Dying Project.

Prologue: There is a Thread
by Suzannah Arnold

Helen Ansley's ninety years have largely been a "what now/what next" lifetime. Born with the century (2-26-1900) she shares its impulses and patterns. From the beginning *"what now"* has always been studying needs in each decade and initiating change. *"What next"* has been finding the most pressing problems and working toward correcting them.

This twentieth century couldn't have found a more likely advocate than Helen to live out and work for the individual "rights" for all people. To be sure, not everyone born in 1900 carries her commitment to researching and implementing action in the world. She has always been on the frontier of change!

For more than twenty years I have studied both Eastern and Western traditions of cycles and patterns, which say that *there is a thread*—a continuum—running through *all life*, a natural, dependable, cyclical thread. And within those cycles are Patterns. Individual patterns, century patterns—patterns everywhere! In fact, I believe that Pattern is Life's gift to us—a true essence to be lived out. It could be called an "assignment".

Helen has lived out her assignment decade by decade, movement by movement, cause by cause, and her current cause, appropriate to this final decade, is the opportunity to achieve a good "conscious" death—at a time, place and in a manner of one's own choosing—and with celebration.

When Helen and I talk about her tireless years and the way she has been driven in her work for people's rights, she asks, "But doesn't everyone think the way I do?"

The answer is "No". Her pattern is unique. She has a "divine discontent". At the present she is busily into the "what now" of death with dignity. But, of course, she is eager to explore her "what next" after death.

The end is a beginning
There is a Thread
A continuum
Celebration!

Suzannah Arnold is a collaborator in the Conscious Living/ Conscious Dying Project, on its Steering Committee, and is sharing the house at 3 Community Road, Belvedere, California, with Helen Ansley.

Helen Green Ansley:
The Pattern of a Century

Helen's personal history parallels the socio-political movements of the century, beginning with the women's suffrage movement in 1910, through wars, depressions, hopes of world government and international peace, the birth of social security, social justice efforts in the 1960s, the development of the human potential and self-actualization movements in the 1970s, research on aging in the 1980s, and now death and dying . . .

• 1900: *A new century, with high hopes for individual rights and the proverbial peace and prosperity*

> Helen Green is born to a liberal family, and is brought up to "leave the world better than you found it . . . "

• The Teens: *World War I; women's rights—education, suffrage and birth control—are major issues*

> HG helps her mother, an active suffragette, distribute pamphlets at age 10; mother invites birth control pioneer Margaret Sanger to speak at church; father on draft board, having to choose who goes to war; brother leaves college to drive an ambulance in

France: HG to Smith College, one of the first women's colleges; active in first college branch of the League of Women Voters

- The '20s: *Post-war economy, and country settles down in peace*
  HG marries Frank Ansley, and they raise two sons

- The '30s: *Depression; rise of Nazism*
  HGA becomes active in Unitarian church as director of junior church, developing a curriculum teaching children how to think rather than what to think; FA works in a bank, and on February 26 (HGA's birthday!) must stand at the bank door and tell depositors that the bank has failed; family completely wiped out

- The '40s: *World War II; the United Nations is born; the stirrings of support for prevention of illness, and for encouragement of mental health*
  HGA helps organize and becomes first president of the Cleveland Council for Mental Health; she is one of the first few women ordnance inspectors; their older son flies bombing missions over Germany; HGA and FA are active with the United World Federalists (UWF), to "develop the United Nations into a limited world federation with

enough power to prevent armed conflict between nations"; they meet UWF president Norman Cousins, and help form the Ohio branch and Cleveland Chapter; their younger son is with the army of occupation in Germany

• The '50s: *The United Nations works to maintain peace around the world; mental health is in the forefront as "snake pits" are exposed*
HGA continues work in mental health, giving lectures on human potential and individuality; she becomes Executive Secretary and then Regional Director for the Mid-Lakes Region of UWF

• The '60s: *Fight for individual freedoms focuses on peace, the draft, segregation, and women's rights; Social Security is enacted in the US*
HGA helps arrange the world meeting of Federalist leaders in San Francisco on the twentieth anniversary of the United Nations; upon retirement from the Lawrence Radiation Laboratory she becomes part-time bookkeeper at the World Without War Council; she is made Administrative Vice-President of the Berkeley League of Women Voters

- The '70s: *The human potential movement is in full swing, as individuals discover their own needs and desires for growth*

    HGA joins advisory board of the Retired Senior Volunteer Program (RSVP); she chairs League of Women Voters' study on Problems and Resources for Aging in Berkeley; she is asked to be one of 12 in the original core group of SAGE (Senior Actualization and Growth Exploration); she is a participant in research on nutrition at the University of California; after the death of her husband she moves to Bellevue, Washington, and co-founds a growth group for seniors

- The '80s: *Holistic health is gaining ground as individuals take responsibility for wellness and positive living—and patients' rights*

    HGA is active as consultant on aging, on joyful living and conscious dying, giving talks and teaching classes

- The '90s: *The final right, the right to die, is now openly discussed*

    HGA moves to Belvedere, California, to work with the Conscious Living/Conscious Dying Project of the Institute of Noetic Sciences; and she sets out to establish a "Way Out Inn"

Life's Finishing School:
A Curriculum For
Living Well

The purpose of life is to leave the world a little better for having lived . . .

My father Frederick Green showed me that the purpose of life is to leave the world a little better for my having lived. He made it clear that because I had a good education, I had a special responsibility to use it for the benefit of those who were not so fortunate.

My family was liberal, and encouraged that in me, with political and philosophical discussion at the dinner table, and visits to the author-philosopher Elbert Hubbard's Roycroft Inn, for lectures, concerts, group walks and hikes, and more discussions.

> *"I am an old man and have had many troubles, but most of them never happened."*
> *—Elbert Hubbard*

This is from the Foreword of Elbert Hubbard's book *An American Bible*, which had—still has—a profound influence on me:

In courts of law, the phrase "I believe" has no standing. Never a witness gives testimony but that he is cautioned thus, "Tell us what you know, not what you believe." In theology, belief has always been regarded as more important than that which your senses say is so.

Almost without exception, "belief" is a legacy, an importation—something borrowed, an echo, and often an echo of an echo. The Creed of the Future will begin "I know", not "I believe". And this creed will not be forced upon the people. . . .

I KNOW:
That I am here in a world where nothing is permanent but change, and that in degree I, myself, can change the form of things and influence a few people;
And that I am influenced by these and other people;
That I am influenced by the example and by the work of men who are no longer alive, and that the work I now do will in degree influence people who may live after my life has changed into other forms;
That a certain attitude of mind and habit of action on my part will add to the peace, happiness and well-being of other people, and that a different thought and action on my part will bring pain and discord to others;
That if I would secure reasonable happiness for myself, I must give out good-will to others;
That to better my own condition I must practice mutuality;
That bodily health is necessary to continued and effective work;
That I am ruled largely by habit;

*That habit is a form of exercise;
That up to a certain point, exercise means
increased strength or ease in effort;
That all life is the expression of spirit;
That my spirit influences my body, and my body
influences my spirit;
That the universe to me is very beautiful, and
everything and everybody in it good and
beautiful, when my body and my spirit are in
harmonious mood;
That my thoughts are hopeful and helpful
unless I am filled with fear, and that to
eliminate fear my life must be dedicated to
useful work—work in which I forget myself;
That fresh air in abundance, and moderate,
systematic exercise in the open air are the part of
wisdom;
That I can not afford, for my own sake, to be
resentful nor quick to take offense;
That happiness is a great power for good, and
that happiness is not possible without
moderation and equanimity;
That time turns all discords into harmony if
men will be kind and patient, and that the
reward which life holds out for work is not
idleness nor rest, nor immunity from work, but
increased capacity, greater difficulties, more
work.*

—Elbert Hubbard

I believe that when we live in the right way, we can feel that we're in harmony . . .

At a religious education conference during the Depression a wonderful minister asked us to write about our own, personal, religion. I wrote:

"I believe that there is a fundamental spirit or power of good in the Universe. This spirit or power I call God.

"I believe that when we live in the right way, we can feel that we're in harmony with that power and are helped and strengthened by it; and that those who feel this radiate the spirit themselves and thus help others. Any honest attempt to live in harmony with God, I call religion.

"I believe that religion is the recognition of simple truths or laws of life which underlie all faiths and which help us to live in harmony with God, the Universe and our fellow man."

Our oldest son Clinton was headed for duty in
the Pacific when the atomic bombs were
dropped on Hiroshima and Nagasaki. I
believed that although something had to be
done to stop this awful war, a bomb was a
horribly wrong use of atomic energy—that
atomic energy could be so useful, but our
government was only thinking of it as a tool for
destruction.

I never worried about the use of nuclear energy
in peacetime; the people I worked with at the
Lawrence Radiation Laboratory were using it
for treating diseases such as cancer, and this I
found acceptable.

But in a room next to my office, scientists were
giving lethal doses of radiation to white mice to
try to learn more about the effects of radiation.
I could see that the animals were being used to
learn things for the benefit of humans, so the
end seemed to justify the means. The
researchers assumed that because the animals
died, human beings subjected to the same
conditions would die too.

This distressed me later as I came to believe
that, as human beings, our attitudes and
thoughts, and those of the people around us,
influence whether we're well or ill.

My peace work taught me how futile it is to
work for peace by being against war; that it's
better to use our energy *for* something rather
than *against* something. We thought of peace
as the presence of law, order and justice,
because unless we had a community that
agreed on the laws of justice and order, we
would never have peace.

*Better to use our energy for something
rather than against something . . .*

Life is a movie . . .

Life is a movie. We are in it. We have to learn to change with each passing scene; if we don't, life passes us by. We become stuck in old, outdated re-runs which are no longer appropriate to our new and present reality.

What was true for us even a short time ago may not be true for us today. Many of us persist in hanging on to old ideas—ideas of how life should be, how we should be, perhaps appropriate for who we were, but not appropriate to where we are and who we are right here, right now.

In 1948 we still had "insane asylums" in Cleveland, and some of us, representing about 30 different churches and women's organizations, formed a mental health council to try to get across an explanation of mental health rather than insanity. I developed a talk to translate the four- and five-syllable words of "psychobabble" that doctors and psychiatrists talk into practical useful terms that everyone could understand, expressing mental health principles in terms of nutrition. It's a way we can talk about how we feel. It revolved around:

The A's and the FFIG's

The **A**'s are the vitamin "emotions". These are the positive emotions that make us feel good:

> **A**musement
>
> **A**cceptance
>
> **A**ppreciation
>
> **A**ffection
>
> **A**chievement

The high calorie **FFIG**'s are the negative "emotions" that upset us:

> **F**ear
>
> **F**rustation
>
> **I**nferiority
>
> **G**uilt

We have to have some of the **FFIG** calories—
they give us energy, they help us grow, and they
give us a push, so we'll go out and do
something, do something about what we're
afraid of, or what we're frustrated with. But if
you get too many **FFIG**'s they can make you
sick.

Our ordinary daily life with its ups and downs
provides a mixed diet of emotions. If we get
enough of the **A**'s we can digest quite a lot of
FFIG's, but sometimes our emotional diet is so
badly out of balance that it affects our work and
our health.

A balanced emotional diet of **A**'s and **FFIG**'s
equals a recipe for happiness.

Amusement:

We need to laugh. As we get older, it sometimes
seems as though we get fewer and fewer
opportunities to laugh, fewer things to laugh at.

Acceptance:

I think the most important thing we need is
acceptance, in a group of people where we have
things in common. We need to "belong", to
associate ourselves with others whose aims and
values are similar to our own. **Acceptance** is
the recognition of things we have in common.

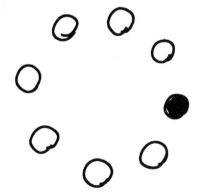

Not to be on top of the heap where you're going to be knocked off all the time. Perhaps it's when you're approaching 65, and may be forced to retire.

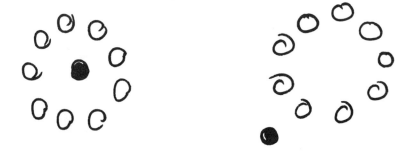

This is the single parent being pulled apart by everything around them, and this is the newcomer, outside.

I think you can see yourself somewhere in all of these.

Appreciation:

We also need **a**ppreciation of the need to feel needed, that we have a particular contribution to make as an individual for the good of the whole.

This includes **a**ppreciation of our differences. There is no one most beautiful flower.

There's no one most important piece in the picture puzzle; without any one the picture would be incomplete. We wouldn't have a picture at all if we weren't all different shapes and sizes and colors, and yet we keep trying to fit ourselves into "the wrong hole", or try to make everybody just the same shape and size.

We're all so self-conscious of where we don't fit in, but we're not conscious of the value of our differences. This is what I've been learning since I was 75.

And if we were all just alike, it would be very dull and uninteresting.

We are not conscious of the value of our
differences . . .

Affection:

Affection is the need to relate ourselves closely to other people so that what happens to us "affects", or concerns, them, and vice versa. It is the need to feel concern for someone other than ourself.

We need **affection**, bonds. I think of the bonds that tie together the mountain climbers— sometimes one's up, sometimes another, but there's something to hold on to.

Affection is the recognition that the happiness of other people is important to us.

Achievement:

We also need a feeling of **achievement**, that we're going somewhere, not round and round in a maze.

Achievement is the need to feel that we have accomplished something by our efforts, that our time, thought and energy have been used for a purpose.

Achievement is the realization that we have succeeded in doing something we started out to do.

We like progress, purpose, goals in life, and I think the most important thing is to feel you have a purpose.

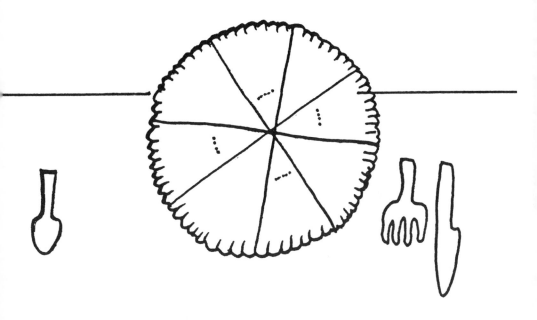

Achievement . . .

The **FFIG**'s:

FFIG's are the emotions which upset us:

Fear

Frustration

Inferiority

Guilt

F_{ear:}

Fear is the emotion that tends to paralyze action and prevent us from using our reason.

We have to think what we are afraid of, and what we can do about it. For example, when I was 75 I fell downstairs and broke my hip, and ever since then when I go downstairs I hold on to something or somebody; that's a very simple one. But I know when I face broad stairs I'm scared. But it doesn't stop me from getting to where I want to go.

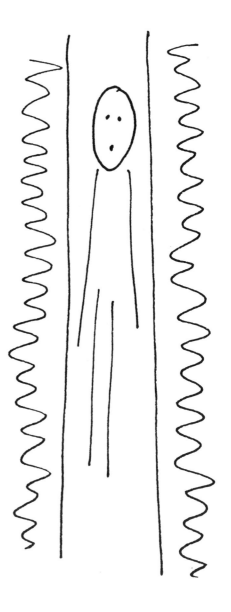

Frustration:

Frustration often makes us strike out blindly at someone we love.

Now you may know the prayer of Alcoholics Anonymous: *God give me the patience to accept what I cannot change, the courage to change what ought to be changed, and the wisdom to know the difference.* Well, there are so many frustrations I see that I can't do anything about, but I'm finding that there are some that I can do something about. And so I try to do something about them.

*Well, there are so many frustrations I see that I
can't do anything about, but I'm finding that
there are some that I can do something about.
And so I try to do something about them . . .*

Inferiority:

Inferiority makes us bossy, critical, hard to live with, because we are trying to show that we are better than someone else.

No one is inferior—we're just different. But the somebodys who are another kind of different want to make themselves feel better, so they try to make us feel inferior.

But we don't want to be just like other people, unless it's somebody we admire a good deal, and that's different.

You don't need to feel inferior. You may find that there is knowledge you want that you see somebody else has—go after it. But that isn't inferiority.

But the somebodys who are another kind of different want to make themselves feel better, so they may try to make us feel inferior . . .

Guilt:

Guilt can send us into a tailspin of depression, and it often makes us avoid the friends and activities that we most enjoy.

Yes, I now know things that I wish I had done differently. But at the time I did the best I knew how, with what I knew. I think this is true even of criminals—they're after something and they don't know how to get it.

For example, I feel guilty now, although I don't need to call it **guilt**, about my son, who is 66, a retired schoolteacher. He's done a grand job, but when he was small, *they* said spare the rod and spoil the child; you weren't supposed to cuddle them. We've learned a lot since about the need for affection, and now I do wish I'd cuddled my son the way my great granddaughter has been cuddled.

Guilt can send us into a tailspin of depression,
and it often makes us avoid the friends and
activities that we most enjoy . . .

"Real guilt is a person's failure to live up to his
own potential."
—Abraham Maslow

What do we do if we get too many **FFIG**'s? We hit or hide, fight or take flight. We feel anger or depression, and either one of them just makes it worse.

If your stomach is upset, if you get too much rich food, too many calories, first you watch your diet, you avoid certain foods, and you reach for a few of the **A**'s—you reach for the chicken soup, and the orange juice, and often you can straighten out your thinking. You call a friend, relax with music. You watch your emotional diet, and deliberately seek out people and situations that supply you with **A**'s and avoid those that give you the **FFIG**'s.

*Seek out people and situations that supply you with **A**'s and avoid those that give you the* ***FFIG**'s . . .*

Looking From All Sides

*List some of the **FFIG**'s that still bother you.
Write a particular example of each of these here
or on a card or piece of paper. Now look at the
other side: Has one of these **FFIG**'s been a gift
as well? Has it spurred you to a new view of, or
action in, life? If you absolutely cannot—yet—
see a positive side to this **FFIG**, please put it
into an iridescent bubble and let it float up and
away from you. You can do it.*

Doctors will give you a pill for depression, and a pill if you feel too high—they don't want you to have those emotions. We need a place where we can release these emotions.

There used to be more grandmothers around living with us, and aunts and uncles that we could talk to. We had larger families, with somehow a more friendly atmosphere in which it was safe to talk.

Co-counseling has been developed to create a safe place to express your emotions. Keep trying—you will find someone who will listen: a friend, a minister. You're important enough to be heard.

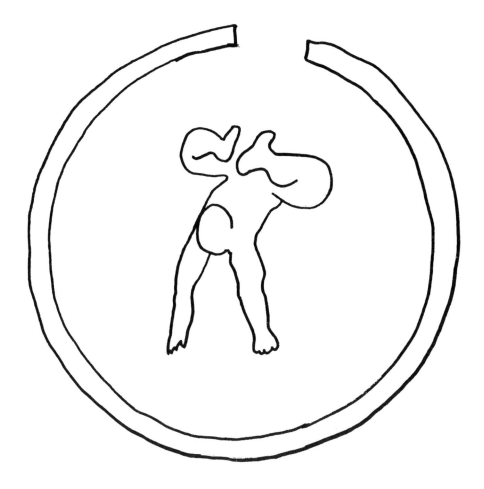

We need a place where we can release these emotions . . .

So the recipe for happiness is a balanced diet of
A's and **FFIG**'s. We cannot control the
emotional diet which is served up to us every
day by those with whom we come in contact, but
we can control the emotions which we offer to
others.

*But we can control the emotions
we offer to others . . .*

And your emotions differ from food in a most
important way: The emotions which we give to
others nourish us as much as the ones which
are given to us.

We may not be lucky enough to be surrounded
by the five **A**'s ourselves, but nothing can
prevent our giving them to those with whom we
come in contact.

The emotions which we give to others nourish us
as much as the ones which are given to us . . .

It's as though you get on an elevator: Which button do you press?

Are you going to think of all the things you can't do, or are you going to think of all the things you can do? All the things that are wrong with the world, or some of the things that are right with the world?

There are people getting on our elevator who insist on pushing the down button.

You can choose to push the up button.

It is as though you get on an elevator. Which button do you press?

There is a destiny
That makes us brothers
No one goes his way alone.
All that we send into the lives of others
Comes back into our own.
—Edwin Markham

Which is simply do onto others as you would
have others do onto you.

Then there's hell and heaven. Hell is a place
with a big big table just laden with all the good
things in life, good experiences and all, but the
men and women seated at that table are gaunt,
starving, unhappy people. They have stretched
their arms so much getting things that now
their arms are too long and they can't get the
food to their mouths.

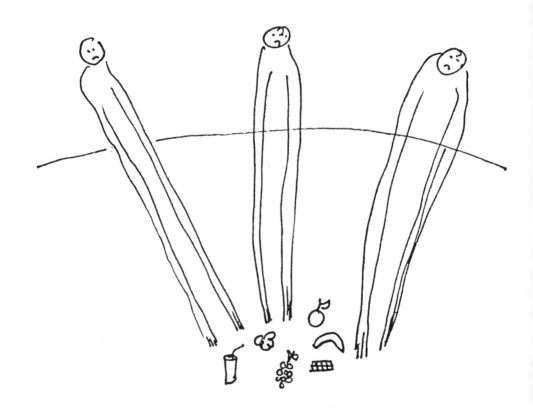

Heaven is a place with a similar table, with all those wonderful things on it. The men and women there also have long arms, but they are happy and healthy—they use their arms to feed each other.

Heaven as you envision it:

My Code of Values

for a **RICH** Life:

R-Responsibillity

I-Integrity

C-Courtesy

H-Humor

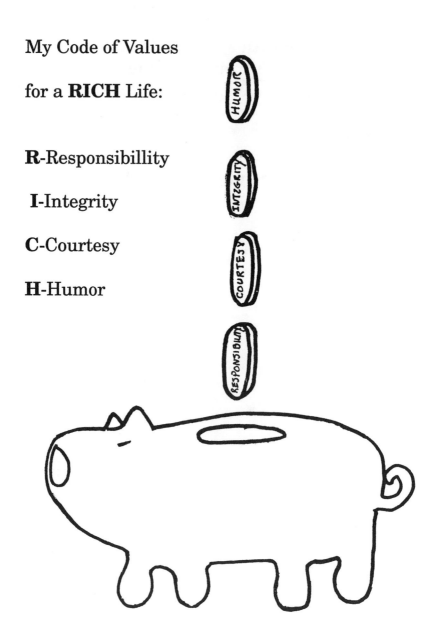

Code of values for a rich life . . .

Growing Wise to Ourselves

In 1973 I chaired a League of Women Voters'
study on Problems and Resources for Aging in
Berkeley. We conducted an extensive survey to
find out what was being done by public and
private agencies, churches and businesses in
Berkeley about the concerns of older people:
health education; death and dying; health
maintenance; safety; financial and legal counseling; illness; loneliness; independence;
income; transportation; mental health; living
arrangements; and recreation.

The answer we discovered: nothing much. It
seemed that if older people were to get any help
at all, they had to be sick. We drew up a list of
suggested needs, and the League began to
monitor federal, state and city government on
its support of senior services and programs.

**From our 1974 report
to the Berkeley League of Women Voters:
"Death and Dying" section:**

"The need to maintain dignity and some control over terminal illness is necessary for calm acceptance of death. There is a great fear of a long, costly and painful illness, and of being kept alive when life has lost all meaning. There is great reluctance on the part of doctors, family and friends to talk frankly with a person who is dying and who may wish to have a voice in final arrangements. Varying religious and legal attitudes toward death and divided public opinion on euthanasia present additional problems.

"Fifty years ago most people died at home in their own beds, and death was a part of our everyday lives. In 1971 only 18.5% of people over 65 who died in Berkeley died at home. An open conversation on death and dying was practically nonexistent.

"Today, however, the subject is being openly discussed on network tv programs, in monthly magazines, in daily newspapers, as well as in lectures, workshops and seminars for medical personnel and theological students. Some colleges and even high schools are now including the subject of death. Crisis counseling for family or patient care is available as is help with preplanning low-cost funerals.

"For those who fear long terminal illness and being kept alive beyond their wishes, copies of a Living Will and a patient's bill of rights and helpful material on euthanasia can be obtained from the Euthanasia Educational Council. There is considerable interest in the idea of a hospice, a nice place to die, patterned after those in England and New Haven, Connecticut."

In 1974 I was invited to be a guinea pig in a study of the effects of the holistic health approach and the modern growth movement—which was popular with many younger people—on people in their sixties, seventies and eighties, as one of the 12 in the original core group of SAGE (Senior Actualization and Growth Exploration), a research project of Gay Luce, with Eugenia Gerrard and Ken Dychtwald. (The program went on to be federally funded by NIMH.) We learned a variety of deep relaxation methods, from biofeedback and massage to breathing exercises, meditation and yoga. We were exposed to music and art therapy and to talks on meditation and psychic healing.

It gave us all a lift to think that we were sages. We were learning so rapidly that everyone was astonished. I believed, however, that when you have years of learning and experiences behind you, you have a background of things to hook new ideas on to, and learning is easier.

SAGE was a wonderful kind of education. We were teaching and learning at the same time by sharing experiences and concepts of a lifetime. The young professionals found us perceptive and quick to learn, contrary to stereotypes of the elderly. They changed their attitudes toward their own aging processes as they shared in our discussions. We, the oldsters, broke out of our own stereotyped ideas of our "declining years"; we were discovering many ways to enjoy our remaining time, rather than just to survive. Our newly learned techniques were practical. They not only helped us cope with personal problems but they also gave us a new self-image.

"Who Am I?"
Establishing Your Own Identity

This is one kind of exercise we did at SAGE that helped us in self-discovery: Sit and relax, the way Marion Weber describes on page 10, then keep repeating the question "Who am I?" After each question write your responses. Now go on from this basic exercise, and recognize each answer for what it is. For example, if I answer "I am Frank's wife", I'd recognize that as "No, that's a social role—Who am I?" Keep asking and answering until you find a very basic pure response.

"Who Am I?" Part Two

Now look at all your answers, and branch out from them. See what is unique and special about this identity. How am I different in this identity from other parts of my life? To my example answer of "I am Frank's wife"—that perhaps wasn't the basic answer to "Who am I?", but it certainly represents part of my life. So for this second part I could say, "My being Frank's wife taught me how to love somebody no matter what."

I remember reading Viktor Frankl's writing back then, about the things that give life meaning and the "ah-ha's" of life. He said that we always have a choice. Most people say, "Oh, no, I had no choice. I just had to do this."

I was learning that we always have a choice in how we react to things that happen to us.

Frankl also wrote about the importance of having a purpose in life. SAGE was becoming the purpose of my life, in a sense, at *this* stage of my life.

The "ah-ha's" of life . . .

You don't blame circumstances.
You take charge . . .

I began to do as author John Gardner suggested:

"Reject the myth that learning is for young people. It's what you learn after you know it all that counts.

"Learn all your life—from your successes, from your failures. When you hit a spell of trouble, ask, 'What is it trying to teach me?' The lessons aren't always happy ones. In one of his essays Ralph Waldo Emerson wrote, 'Bad times have a scientific value. These are occasions a good learner would not miss.'

"The things you learn in maturity seldom involve information and skills. You learn to bear with the things you can't change. You learn to avoid self-pity. You learn not to burn up energy in anxiety. You learn that most people are neither for you nor against you but rather are thinking about themselves. You learn that no matter how much you try to please, some people are never going to like you—a notion that troubles at first but is eventually relaxing.

"One of the most valuable things you learn is that ultimately you're the one who's responsible for you. You don't blame others. You don't blame circumstances. You take charge."

In 1974 I volunteered to be a guinea pig again, along with six other people over age 65, for research on nutrition at the University of California headed by Professor Sheldon Margen. The study proved that we were healthier than the researchers expected of old people, and that we could live on vitamins and certain nutrition.

This was the first time the sponsor, a major cereal company, had done any controlled research on nutrition and older people. Being involved with this started a whole new interest in nutrition for me.   Since then I've read everything I could find on the subject.

I learned a lot about hospitals and nursing homes because of Frank's experience in two of each. I even changed doctors when one said, "At his age, what difference does it make?" Frank died two years after our fiftieth wedding anniversary.

I learned about the Living Will, cremation, simple funerals, insurance settlements, Medicare and Social Security forms, and what it's like to be a widow.

Seed

*Charlene Harman visited our Conscious Living/
Conscious Dying Steering Committee and told of
her work with the Palo Alto version of SAGE
(which they call PASSAGE). This is an exercise
she said is very inspiring (her group did it with
music and dance, but if you would rather you
could just imagine and perhaps write—or
draw!—your impressions): Pretend you are a
seed, dropped into a wonderful piece of earth.
Curl up and be a seed. The first bit of stem
starts to emerge, then breaks through the earth.
It grows and grows up into the light. It
branches, and buds, then blooms and flowers
and then seeds, and then starts to move back
into the earth.*

In 1975, I fell and broke my hip, but I got a new steel one and healed very quickly, in just six weeks.

When I was in the hospital Gay Luce brought astronaut Edgar Mitchell, the sixth man to walk on the moon, in to see me. He had become very involved in founding the Institute of Noetic Sciences, which is an organization devoted to the exploration of human consciousness. The Institute helped Gay with some pilot funding for her research.

I joined the Institute, and a letter from me in its first *Noetic Sciences Bulletin* began a correspondence which eventually resulted in the setting up of the Conscious Living/ Conscious Dying Project exactly fifteen years after my meeting Mitchell.

When I got out of the hospital, I moved to an apartment in Bellevue, Washington, still driving my (1964) Dodge Dart, and began an active new career as Consultant on Aging, giving talks, attending workshops, and teaching classes on the New Image of Aging, stressing the dignity and worth of the individual and the link between the body and the mind.

As Rabbi Raphael Levine said about aging (in a chapter about me in his book *Profiles in Service*), "This is a facet of Oriental culture: After lives of work, the elderly commit themselves to attaining enlightenment through meditation and study; they are at leisure to sit at the feet of a spiritual master and ponder his wisdom."

Well, we didn't spend much time sitting at anyone's feet, but we were learning that we have minds and spirits, that we're not just old bodies.

Telos—old age is a time of fulfillment . . .

Joy Carey, who had taken some training from SAGE, said to me, "Helen, let's start something like SAGE up here!" And so we did. We wanted to give our new class a name, but we didn't want to repeat the name SAGE. No name was forthcoming, so Joy said she'd meditate on it.

When she went to bed one night, she said to herself, "I've got to have a name for our program in the morning." When she awoke the word "Telos" was in her mind, but she didn't know what it meant.

One of the participants' sons had studied Greek, and he told us that Telos means fulfillment, or, to be fulfilled. That was perfect for us. It symbolized the goal of the program—to increase the perception that old age is a time of fulfillment, the season of harvest, the richest and most valuable time of all, an unusual concept for modern American society.

We still use the symbol of the oak tree because the telos of an acorn is the oak tree.

What Do I Value?

Go down the list and check those values that seem the most important now in your life. Are there others missing from the list? Add these, too. Of those checked, mark the most important with an "A", and the less important with a "B".

    Achievement
    Appreciation of Beauty
    Appreciation of Others
    Cooperation
    Creativity
    Emotional Well-Being
    Freedom
    Health
    Honesty
    Justice
    Knowledge
    Love
    Loyalty
    Morality
    Physical Appearance
    Pleasure
    Power
    Recognition
    Religion / Spirituality
    Skill
    Wealth
    Wisdom

Your Legacy

A new discovery! If you could bottle whatever is most important to you and give it away—what would it be? Look through your list of values and see what you would like made into an elixir that could be available to the whole world. Why is it important for others to have this, do you think?

Another Legacy

Congratulations! You have been given an incredible, uncountable sum of money that could be used to carry on your goals, in your name, after your death. What would you like to have done with your money?

Through the years I have discovered that rather than studying old age, doctors merely study the diseases that accompany aging. But doctors do the only thing they know how to do, I guess.

And we have found that at least 80 percent of the older people don't need looking after. Their problems are the same as in the rest of the population, and they should be helping with those problems, not saying, "Look, you take care of us".

But many of the limitations associated with age are often self-imposed in reaction to prevailing cultural mores and are not necessary.

I hope we're going to break society's mold around old people. The researchers keep studying sick people to find out what's wrong instead of healthy ones who must done have something right!

It is time to do research on the older people in society who are healthy, hale and hearty instead of those who are already in a state of dis-ease.

I would like to see research on why some people become more useful, have a greater sense of purpose and contribute more in later life.

And as you'll see in the other half of this book, I have some pretty strong opinions about dying.

As the cells in my body renew
And my purpose in life I review
I find, growing older,
I'm now growing bolder
And increasingly hard to subdue!

*"Whether you think you can or think you can't,
you're right."*
—*Henry Ford*

*"Within yourself lies the cause of whatever enters
into your life. To come into the full realization
of your own awakened interior powers, is to be
able to condition your life in exact accord with
what you would have it.*

*"The optimist is right. The pessimist is right.
The one differs from the other as the light from
the dark. Yet both are right. Each is right from
his own particular point of view, and this point
of view is the determining factor in the life of
each. It determines as to whether it is a life of
power or of impotence, of peace or of pain, of
success or of failure. The optimist has the power
of seeing things in their entirety and in their
right relations. The pessimist looks from a
limited and a one-sided point of view. The one
has his understanding illumined by wisdom, the
understanding of the other is darkened by
ignorance. Each is building his world from
within, and the result of the building is
determined by the point of view of each. The
optimist, by his superior wisdom and insight, is
making his own heaven, and in the degree he
makes his own heaven is he helping to make one
for all the world beside. The pessimist, by virtue
of his limitations, is making his own hell, and
in the degree that he makes his own hell is he
helping to make one for all mankind."*
                                        —Ralph Waldo Trine

I grew up with this image of aging, and maybe
you did too: You're born, you go to school, you
get a job, you get married, get a family, life
begins at 40, then maturity, when you enjoy
success; then there's 65 and old age, and from
there on you're supposed to go down. And that
in a way is what our culture has been telling us,
isn't it?

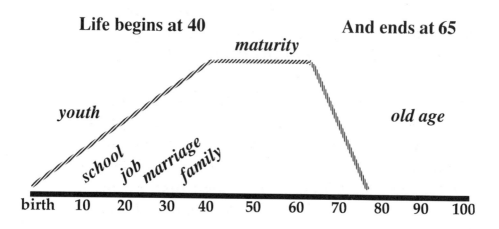

What is your general view of aging?

birth 10 20 30 40 50 60 70 80 90 100

Whereas, when I made a time chart for my own life—

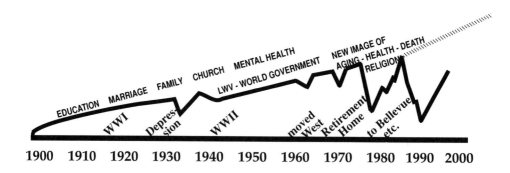

I was born in 1900, and in 1914 there was
World War I. I got married, and had a family.
Then we had the Depression and we lost
everything—I was scared to death about that
time.

But gradually we came back up, and I got into
church work, and League of Woman Voters, and
then Mental Health. I met Norman Cousins and
became active in the United World Federalists
working for world government.

So I've gotten my education, my philosophy,
from all of these ups and downs, and working
with wonderful people, and my two sons.

I didn't die at any of these places when I
thought I would, I didn't starve to death.
Something happened—each time I'd find a new
purpose in life, something to work for.

List your own ups and downs:

*and mark your ups and downs
on your own graph:*

1900   1910   1920   1930   1940   1950   1960   1970   1980   1990   2000

Now I have this new image of aging: growth,
maturity, wisdom—and you grow into death.

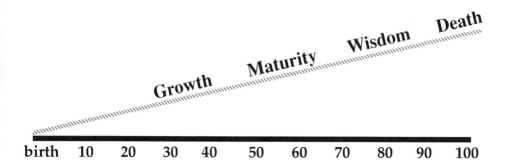

What is your image of aging now?
Perhaps it's not a graph at all:

birth   10   20   30   40   50   60   70   80   90   100

NEW IMAGE OF AGING
Becoming a Whole Person

We're the target — being pulled apart by the people who are trying to help us

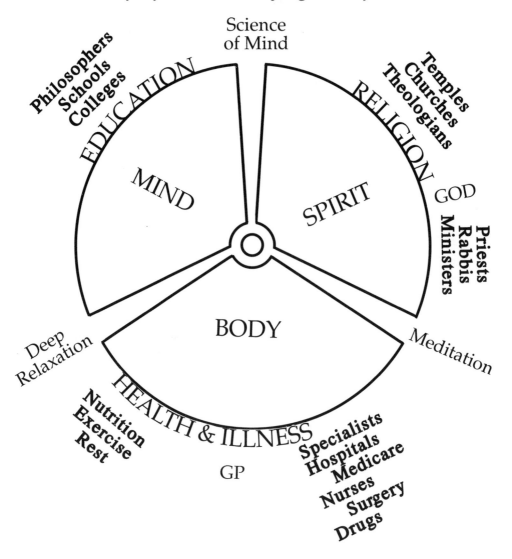

Here is what happens, I've found: We are the target, being pulled apart by the people who are trying to help us—people in the fields of education, or religion, or health and illness.

Doctors think about illness rather than health; they become specialists rather than trying to put us together. Even the different churches don't agree (except the Unitarians, they try to take in everybody).

We are in the center—everybody gives us different advice, and then gets mad if we don't take it.

Granted there are people who aren't like that at all, but there are many who think that they know The Way. I just know that anybody who knows The Way is wrong, because there is no one way. We each are different and have to have our *own* way.

NEW IMAGE OF AGING
Becoming a Whole Person

Taking responsibility for ourselves
Reaching a balance

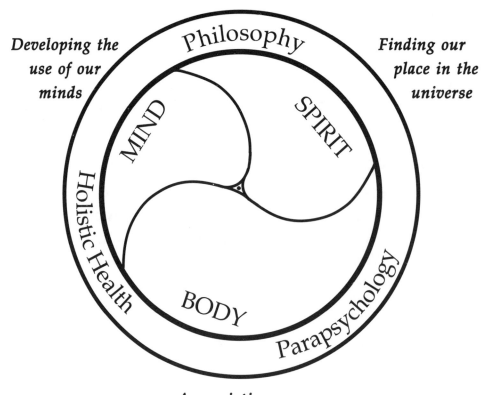

Developing the use of our minds

Finding our place in the universe

Appreciating our wonderful bodies